A+ books

DROUGHTS

BE AWARE AND PREPARE

by Martha E. H. Rustad

Consultant:
Joseph M. Moran, PhD
Meteorology, Professor Emeritus
University of Wisconsin-Green Bay

CAPSTONE PRESS
a capstone imprint

A+ Books are published by Capstone Press,
1710 Roe Crest Drive, North Mankato, Minnesota 56003
www.capstonepub.com

Library of Congress Cataloging-in-Publication Data
Rustad, Martha E. H. (Martha Elizabeth Hillman), 1975–
 Droughts : be aware and prepare / by Martha E. H. Rustad ; editor, Jill Kalz.
    pages cm — (A+ books. Weather aware)
 Summary: "Describes how droughts form, their effects, and how people can prepare for them"—Provided
by publisher.
 Includes index.
 Audience: K-3.
 ISBN 978-1-4765-9905-2 (library binding)
 ISBN 978-1-4765-9910-6 (eBook PDF)
1. Droughts—Juvenile literature. 2. Drought forecasting—Juvenile literature. I. Kalz, Jill. II. Title.
 QC929.25.R87 2015
 551.57'73—dc23   2014006645

Editorial Credits
Jill Kalz, editor; Lori Bye, designer; Svetlana Zhurkin, media researcher; Tori Abraham, production specialist

Photo Credits
Library of Congress, 15; Shutterstock: Alison Hancock, cover (inset), borsvelka (background), back cover and
throughout, Croato, 1, Dave Weaver, 3 (middle right), 22, Denise Lett, 24, DFAagaard, 2 (middle left), 8–9, Fabio
Alcini, 20, James Mattil, 2 (right), 16, Karen Kaspar, 3 (right), 25, MarcusVDT, 27, Martin Lisner, 2 (middle right),
11, Matej Hudovernik, 21, mironov, 17, Monkey Business Images, 26, moomsabuy, 14, Mr Pics, 23, mrivserg,
12–13, muratart, 3 (left), 18 (inset), Oleksandr Pastukh, 3 (middle left), 28–29, Samart Mektippachai, 2 (left), 4,
SP-Photo, 18–19, Stuart Monk, 21 (inset), Vasiliy Merkushev, 10, Yaromir, 6–7, Zurijeta, 5; SuperStock: Science
Faction/Jim Reed, cover

Note to Parents, Teachers, and Librarians
This Weather Aware book uses full-color photographs and a nonfiction format to introduce the concept
of droughts. *Droughts: Be Aware and Prepare* is designed to be read aloud to a pre-reader or to be read
independently by an early reader. Photographs help listeners and early readers understand the text and
concepts discussed. The book encourages further learning by including the following sections: Table of
Contents, Critical Thinking Using the Common Core, Glossary, Read More, Internet Sites, and Index.
Early readers may need assistance using these features.

Printed in the United States of America in North Mankato, Minnesota
032014   008087CGF14

TABLE OF CONTENTS

BE WEATHER AWARE

Most of the time, we know what the weather will do. It follows a pattern. But sometimes the pattern changes. To keep yourself safe, be weather aware. Here you'll learn about droughts so you can better prepare for them.

WHAT IS A DROUGHT?

A drought takes place over a long period of time. It happens when an area gets less precipitation than usual. Rain, snow, hail, and slect are forms of precipitation. Over time the land dries up. Winds may blow away soil.

Location of Earth's Water

frozen   lakes, rivers, and groundwater

oceans

WHAT CAUSES DROUGHTS?

Changes in Earth's water cycle cause droughts. The water cycle is the movement of water around the planet. It starts with the sun. The sun heats the water at the surface of the ocean, lakes, and rivers. Heat turns the liquid water into a gas. This process is called evaporation.

The newly formed water vapor rises. It joins water vapor given off by plants through transpiration. The water vapor cools and condenses into clouds. From clouds, rain or other precipitation falls to Earth's surface. Water then finds its way into the ocean, lakes, and rivers, and the cycle continues.

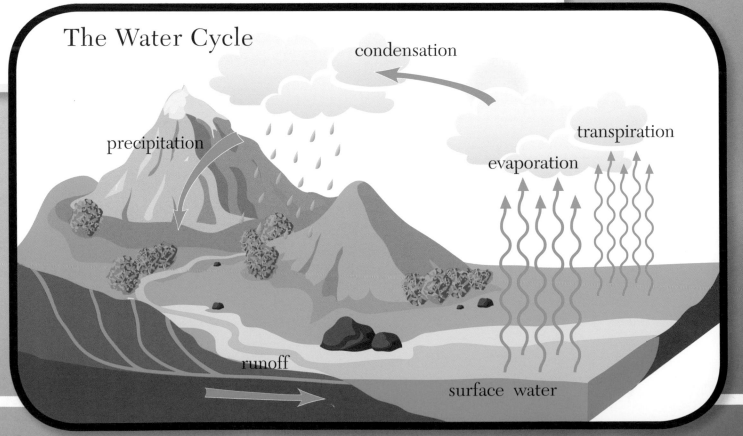

The Water Cycle

condensation

transpiration

precipitation

evaporation

runoff

surface water

Many things may cause a change in the water cycle. Winds high above Earth's surface might shift. Water moving within the ocean may take a different path. Temperatures may unexpectedly rise or fall. These changes can cause less precipitation to fall.

11

A drought forms slowly over weeks or months. Water levels in rivers and lakes drop. Ponds and wetlands dry up. Plants turn brown and brittle. Over time, water deep underground disappears. Wells go dry.

WHERE DO DROUGHTS FORM?

Droughts form in places that get less rain or snow than usual.

High temperatures often come with droughts. In the 1930s, a terrible, hot drought hit the United States. People called it the Dust Bowl because the dry soil turned to dust.

WHY ARE DROUGHTS DANGEROUS?

Fires start easily during droughts. Without water, plants dry up. A spark from lightning or a campfire can set fire to dry trees and grasses. Wildfires spread fast over dry land.

Farmers use irrigation to water crops during droughts. In the driest places, crops grow only with help from irrigation.

Farmers need water to grow
crops. Too little rainfall may kill
fruits, vegetables, and grains.
People and animals may not have
enough to eat because of a drought.

All living things need water to drink. But people also need water to cook and to stay clean. They build dams on rivers to make power for homes. Less water means less power. During a drought, prices for food and power may rise.

Water makes up more than half of the human body. To stay healthy, drink about eight cups of water every day.

HOW DO PEOPLE PREPARE FOR A DROUGHT?

Meteorologists study weather patterns. They keep track of changes. They warn people when droughts might happen. They let firefighters know when wildfires may break out.

To prepare for a drought, cities store water in large holding areas. They may limit water for some uses, such as watering lawns.

Farmers store water for irrigation. They plant crops that need less water. Other people collect rain in special barrels. They use it to water gardens and yards.

You can help save water by using less at home. Turn off the water when you brush your teeth. Take short showers instead of baths. Run the dishwasher only when it's full. Wear your clothes more than once for less laundry.

A drought doesn't end with just one rainstorm. The land may need lots of time to get back to normal.

Droughts are a natural part of our world's weather. They can be dangerous and cause many problems. But you can prepare by saving water and being weather aware.

CRITICAL THINKING USING THE COMMON CORE

1. Explain the basic parts of Earth's water cycle, using the diagram on page 10. (Key Ideas and Details)

2. Describe how droughts can be dangerous. (Craft and Structure)

3. Explain the steps you would take at your home to prepare for a drought. (Integration of Knowledge and Ideas)

GLOSSARY

condense (kuhn-DENS)—to change from a gas to a liquid

dam (DAM)—a wall that stretches across a river; it slows down the rushing water and raises the water level behind it

evaporation (i-vap-uh-RAY-shun)—the process of changing from a liquid to a gas

irrigation (ihr-uh-GAY-shun)—supplying water to crops using a system of pipes and channels

meteorologist (mee-tee-ur-AWL-uh-jist)—a person who studies and predicts the weather

precipitation (pri-sip-i-TAY-shun)—water that falls from the clouds in the form of rain, snow, sleet, or hail

transpiration (transs-puh-RAY-shun)—the process by which plants give off moisture

water cycle (WAH-tur SY-kuhl)—how water changes as it travels around the world and moves between the ground and the air

water vapor (WAH-tur VAY-pur)—water in gas form

READ MORE

Cunningham, Kevin. *Surviving Droughts and Famines.* Natural Disasters. Chicago: Raintree, 2012.

Garland, Sherry. *Voices of the Dust Bowl.* Gretna, La.: Pelican Pub. Co., 2012.

Purdie, Kate. *Sunshine and Drought.* Weatherwise. New York: PowerKids Press, 2010.

INTERNET SITES

FactHound offers a safe, fun way to find Internet sites related to this book. All of the sites on FactHound have been researched by our staff.

Here's all you do:

Visit *www.facthound.com*

Type in this code: 9781476599052

 Check out projects, games and lots more at **www.capstonekids.com**

INDEX